POUND RIDGE LIB
271 Westchester Ave
Pound Ridge,New York
10576-1714
W9-CIH-597

Really Funny Riddles

by Judy A. Winter

Consulting Editor: Gail Saunders-Smith, PhD

CAPSTONE PRESS
a capstone imprint

Pebble Books are published by Capstone Press,
1710 Roe Crest Drive, North Mankato, Minnesota 56003.
www.capstonepub.com

Books published by Capstone Press are manufactured with paper containing at least 10 percent post-consumer waste.

Library of Congress Cataloging-in-Publication Data
Winter, Judy A., 1952–
Really funny riddles / by Judy A. Winter.
p. cm.—(Pebble books. Joke books)
Includes bibliographical references.
Summary: "Simple text and photographs present riddles"—Provided by publisher.
ISBN 978-1-4296-5269-8 (library binding)
1. Riddles, Juvenile. I. Title. II. Series.
PN6371.5.W56 2011
818'.602—dc22 2010029081

Editorial Credits
Gillia Olson, editor; Gene Bentdahl, designer; Sarah Schuette, studio specialist; Marcy Morin, studio scheduler; Laura Manthe, production specialist

Photo Credits
Barbara O'Brien, cover (sheep, bunny), 4 (bunny), 10, 16; Capstone Studio: Karon Dubke, cover (pirate) 6, 8 (mice in cone), 12 (person, toilet), 14, 18, 20, 22: Shutterstock: Dan Collier, 12 (grass hill), DenisNata, 8 (cat), Ericlefrancias, cover (airplane), 4 (airplane)

Note to Parents and Teachers

The Joke Books set supports English language arts standards related to reading a wide range of print for personal fulfillment. Early readers may need assistance to read some of the words and to use the Table of Contents, Read More, and Internet Sites sections of this book.

Printed in the United States of America in North Mankato, Minnesota.
012012 006536CGVMI

Table of Contents

How do bunnies travel?

In a hareplane.

Which stories do bunnies like best?

Ones with hoppy endings.

What do lazy dogs do for fun?

Chase parked cars.

What's the special at the pet shop today?

Buy one dog,
get one flea.

What does a cat like to eat in the summer?

A mice cream cone.

What did the 300-pound mouse say?

Here kitty, kitty.

What did the chicken say when it laid a square egg?

Ouch!

What do you call a chicken at the North Pole?

Lost.

Why did the toilet roll down the hill?

To get to the bottom.

What did one burp say to the other burp?

Let's sneak out the other end.

OWING
24/7
ROADSIDE SERVICE
VEHICLE # 607

What did the dancer do when she hurt her foot?

She called a toe truck.

How do you make a tissue dance?

Put a little boogie in it.

What do you get when you cross a skunk and a sheep?

A woolly animal that smells baaaad.

How much is a skunk worth?

A scent.

3:50 7:00 10:00
5:00 7:30 10:00
4:15 7:15 10:15

Why couldn't the pirate get into the movie?

It was rated Aarrrr.

Where can you find a pirate's bathroom?

On the poop deck.

What do you call a monster with a banana in each ear?

Nothing. He can't hear you.

What do you call a zipper on a banana?

A fruit fly.

Who granted the fish's wish?

The Fairy Cod Mother.

What do you call a fairy that hasn't taken a shower?

Stinkerbell.

Read More

Dahl, Michael. *The Funny Farm: Jokes about Dogs, Cats, Ducks, Snakes, Bears, and Other Animals.* Michael Dahl Presents Super Funny Joke Books. Minneapolis: Picture Window Books, 2011.

Ziegler, Mark. *Mind Knots: A Book of Riddles.* Read It! Joke Books—Supercharged! Minneapolis: Picture Window Books, 2006.

Internet Sites

FactHound offers a safe, fun way to find Internet sites related to this book. All of the sites on FactHound have been researched by our staff.

Here's all you do:

Visit *www.facthound.com*

Type in this code: 9781429652698

Check out projects, games and lots more at **www.capstonekids.com**

Word Count: 243 **Grade:** 1

Early-Intervention Level: 20